EATS, CHEATS

AND

LEAVES

First published 2012 by Fast-Print Publishing of Peterborough, England.

FastPrint
Publishing

www.fast-print.net/store.php

EATS, CHEATS AND LEAVES
Copyright in verse © Jane Bailey 2012
Copyright in illustrations © Gemma Hastilow 2012

ISBN: 978-178035-423-1

An environmentally friendly book printed and bound in England by www.printondemand-worldwide.com

Mixed Sources
Product group from well-managed
forests, and other controlled sources
www.fsc.org Cert no. TT-COC-002641
© 1996 Forest Stewardship Council
FSC

PEFC Certified
This product is
from sustainably
managed forests
and controlled
sources
www.pefc.org
PEFC
PEFC/16-33-415

This book is made entirely of chain-of-custody materials

EATS, CHEATS

AND

LEAVES

How to deal with your
philandering cad

by

Jane Bailey

Illustrations

Gemma Hastilow

EATS, CHEATS AND LEAVES

It isn't just men who're unfaithful,
Some women are equally bad,
But this booklet is written
For women once bitten
By the classic philandering cad.

Part 1:

In which you seek out MR RIGHT *whilst trying to bypass*
MESSIEURS WRONG *and* RAT

Beware all you girls fair and tender,
Heed a story that's older than time:
Don't stop in your fight
To find Mr Right,
But listen a while to this rhyme.

Young girls are hard-wired for affection,
It isn't some time-honoured duty;
We are planning that 'yes'
And that special white dress
From the time we first hear *Sleeping Beauty*.

Now some men are bold and romantic
And some seem to live just for sport,
Some simply want bedding,
And some want a wedding,
Whilst some run a mile at the thought.

There are men who exalt in their freedom,
Some are giving and care about others,
There are tit men and bum men
And then there are some men
Who just want to live with their mothers.

The ones to look out for are cunning:
All those flowers mean there's something to hide.
If he's willing and charming,
So sweet it's disarming,
You can bet there's a bit on the side.

PART 2

In which you discover his TREACHERY *and feel pretty furious, and somewhat stupid*

When he constantly preens in the mirror,
And looks at the back of his hair,
When he seeks your advice
Asking, 'Does this look nice?'
It's a sure sign of his new affair.

When he suddenly closes his lap-top
As you come in to show him your dress,
When one unknown female
Crops up in each email
He's certainly not playing chess.

Friends wonder how you didn't spot things:
How didn't you notice his lechery?
Why didn't you know while
You charged up his mobile,
It held all the clues to his treachery?

Your judgement was clouded by loving
As he sweet-talked his way through your doubts,
And it's easy to miss
The scent in a kiss
When you're busy preparing his sprouts.

And what is so wrong with believing
That love conquers all in the end?
So you cocked up with Dickhead,
But it would be wicked
To think that your heart cannot mend.

You may have tried hard not to show it,
Kept your chin up, smiled brightly and laughed,
But although grieving varies,
Denying that there is
A need for some weeping is daft.

PART 3:

In which you feel pathetically SORRY FOR YOURSELF

He took her on weekends to Paris,
With candlelit meals and champagne,
While you had to make do
With fish fingers or stew
And stay home with the children again.

He was a stranger to nappies and Calpol,
Your nights without sleep were invention;
He'd've rather been dead
Than get up out of bed
To give Sugar-Free Infant Suspension.

The number of times that he worked late,
Coming home to your tender embrace;
If you'd noticed that packet
Tucked away in his jacket,
He'd've had shepherd's pie in his face.

Remember the nights that you waited,
Afraid of a car crash or worse?
Now you know if that lecher
Had been on a stretcher
He would just have made out with the nurse.

Remember the kids thought they'd lost him
On the beach down in Devon? Far from it:
He turned up all 'cross'
At that call from his 'boss' -
It's enough to make anyone vomit.

And each holiday seemed to be broken
By a curious threat of the sack
If he missed a work meeting
(i.e. overnight cheating):
It's so obvious now, looking back.

His mum disapproved of the marriage;
She'd have stopped it if only he'd let her.
It was really bad timing
For her social climbing:
(Her son could've done a lot better).

He's robbed you of all of those memories,
The photograph albums are savage:
Though you're smiling together,
You now wonder whether
He's dreaming of leaving the marriage.

Remember those dinners with couples?
It's a shame, but try not to feel slighted.
Endure break-up chatter
Whilst nibbling ciabatta?
Who can blame them that you're not invited?

His earnings are hidden from view now
(Though he seems to be making a mint),
For he's gone self-employed
And you're really annoyed
When the CSA tell you he's skint.

The children look lost and bewildered,
Their family's falling apart.
He says mindless stuff
Like, 'Kids are quite tough,'
But their sadness is breaking your heart.

You repeatedly tell them he loves them,
(They think *they're* why he chose not to stay),
But if what you say's true
Then it has to be you:
You've driven their father away.

You've hit insecurity meltdown.
Were your abs not as tight as required?
Did you have rancid breath?
Did you bore him to death?
Was your lingerie just a bit 'tired'?

Were you lacking in funny one-liners?
Did you not do your housework efficiently?
Was his ego not flattered?
Was that all that mattered?
Were your muffins not buttered sufficiently?

When the chaos he's caused just eludes him,
Though one child's self-harming in rage,
And the other's not eating,
But he keeps repeating,
'That's normal in children their age';

When he tells you he really did love you,
And your cooking was second to none,
But there's no point in blaming
The girl you are naming,
It's just that you stopped being 'fun';

(But fun is quite hard to keep going
When your lecherous man's never there.
There's no use in nagging:
He's worn out with shagging,
So earth-moving moments are rare);

Then be happy that he's buggered off now,
Or maybe you showed him the door.
Changing leopards are risible,
Those spots are still visible:
He's not coming back any more.

PART 4:

In which you feel so jolly angry you want to do him an INJURY, *but fortunately rise above it*

You dreamt often of physical injury
And guiltily thought of castration,
And you sorely lamented
Double-glazing prevented
The option of defenestration.

He tells you it's time to 'move on' now,
Though he understands how you are feeling.
If he'd just put his heels
In front of your wheels
Moving on would be very appealing.

But no one would say you're vindictive
And there's only so much you can grieve,
So when love is souring
It's very empowering
To have a few tricks up your sleeve.

PART 5:

In which you find ways to STOP BEING A VICTIM

He's left all his suits in the wardrobe;
You wonder he's got such a nerve,
But wait a mo - wowsers! -
There's cash in those trousers,
And a mini-break's what you deserve.

Don't cut off the sleeves of his jackets,
It's demeaning, you're better than that.
Pack the lot while you're seething,
There's nothing like leaving
Twelve bin-bags on Oxfam's front mat.

You can clear out his sweaty old tee-shirts
And the dumb-bells that he didn't use;
You can jump into bed
With a good book instead
And take as much room as you choose.

It's wonderful driving without him,
Not having to sit clenching jaws,
Not hearing him snap
That you can't read a map
And his driving is better than yours.

And you don't have to drive him from parties,
He can drink what he likes and go stick it.
You can drive where you please
Without his CDs
And you don't have to listen to cricket.

His tool-kit is still in the toolshed,
Used once for that wonky old shelf.
Don't give that home-wrecker
His old Black-and-Decker
But learn how to use it yourself.

There are bits of old tree in the garage
From his wood-turning, never completed.
Introduce this small trove
To a wood-burning stove,
Then at least you're sustainably heated.

Maybe call all those women he slept with
(There was certainly quite a collection);
Would they think you a cynic
Suggesting a clinic
For Sexually Transmitted Infection?

You feel a bit sad over Christmas,
But you won't have to watch how you tread,
And you won't have to wrap
All that Christmassy crap
For in-laws who wish you were dead.

Your children will listen to phone calls;
They'll hear you grief-stricken and cross.
You tried not to show it
But now that they know it,
They want you to show him who's boss.

They tell you they don't want a doormat,
They tell you to stop being kind.
'If *we* make a fuss
He get's angry with *us,*
So give him a piece of your mind!'

Your eldest may find compensations,
For though he's still missing that louse,
He delights in the notion
Of hidden promotion
To Adult Mark Two in the house.

Now take a long look in the mirror:
It's that grief-stricken look which offends.
For one, it's not pretty
And two, your self-pity
Is boring the pants off your friends.

If it seems like your life is in pieces,
Just focus on all the new perks:
You know you've been waiting
To try online dating
And now you can see if it works.

So you're seen with a Matt then a Harry,
And with Anton you cause quite a rumour.
When your friends call around
At least you'll be found
With a man with a Good Sense of Humour.

It's so good to be emailed and courted,
Though dating was never your thing.
So he isn't The One,
You can still have some fun,
And there's nothing so wrong with a fling.

You've filled up his drawers with silk knickers:
If he's back for his novelty socks,
The new male contenders
Who glimpse those suspenders
Will be helping you change all the locks.

And after a spell with the dating,
Your social life's vibrant and active.
Though not totally cured
You should feel reassured:
There are men who still find you attractive.

So now you can try out Flamenco,
And woodwork or Art could be good.
Night classes are waiting,
Forget all that dating,
You just want to dabble in wood.

Or why don't you set up a book group?
Unravel the conflict and plot?
With slim sticks of carrot
Discuss *Flaubert's Parrot*
And whether you like it or not?

Get down and get dirty with Lawrence,
Smile wryly at literary jokes;
Look sultry and clever
With William Trevor,
Recline with Sebastian Faulks.

CONCLUSION:

In which you realise what a dick he was and FEEL GOOD
ABOUT THE FUTURE

If you still feel betrayed and abandoned,
Put your chin up and listen to me:
What you found out last summer
Has been a real bummer,
But knowing the TRUTH sets you FREE.

Although it is wise to be cautious,
Don't let that bad apple defeat you.
There are men who are kind,
And you may even find
There's a good one just waiting to meet you.

He's ferociously clever and handsome,
And he doesn't think loyalty's silly;
Were it all up to you,
Corgi-registered too,
Although maybe that's gilding the lily.

So come all of you maids fair and tender
(Though your maidenhead's gone for a burton),
If each morning on waking,
Your heart isn't aching,
Then you're making good progress for certain.

When he says he can't pay for the children,
When he says that he's run out of luck,
Don't strangle the fella,
But write a best-seller,
And tell him you don't give a f...!

JANE BAILEY

Jane is the author of four novels, including *Tommy Glover's Sketch of Heaven* (Constable & Robinson 2005) and *Mad Joy* (Constable & Robinson 2006). She heard it was hard to find an uplifting self-help book on this subject, so decided to write one. Somehow it came out in rhyme.

www.jane-bailey.co.uk

GEMMA HASTILOW

Gemma is an illustrator and cartoonist living and working in Cheltenham. She has been drawing funny pictures for children and grown-ups for as long as she can remember.
She is getting married next year but will be keeping her fingers crossed.......

www.gemmahastilow.com